YOU'RE WELCOME

Sharnice Miles

I said this life is hard. She said the beauty is in the struggle...

©sharnice miles

lotus flower	8
the mind of a man	10
love like…	12
his faith	14
he is…	15
my morning	17
a flower in God's garden …	18
zion	20
the phoenix	21
you are…	23
experiencing him	25
I fear	26
that's the way it goes	28
when love dies…	30
when he leaves…	32
he left.	34
I gave you	35
alive, wild and free	38
where I want to be	39
we forget	40
alive and wild and…	41
firefly	42
you	43

when they see us - one   45

we are   47

when they see us - two   48

you fear   50

when they see us - three   52

the black experience   54

self-reflection   57

He became the cool breeze in a not so hot summer...

lotus flower

Beyond the horizon
Far past the sun
On the borderline of God's land
A lotus flower, traveling through mud and found the light
Me... a mer plaything in God's hand
Me... a mer flower in Gods garden, often wondering when will be my time?
When will my time come?
When will the bells ring? Or have they already been rung?
WHAT is God's plan for me?
What does he have in mind?

I walked on the land of equivocation
Imagination runs wild in the heart of man
But substances of reality vibrates through the sand and patterns form
Ruled by the world we form
Consciously making unconscious decisions
In this dimension, chaos is the norm
And with the storm... we transfer into something lukewarm
Something apathetic then apologetic then pleasing
Something gentle

I love Singing songs that's already been sung
And the taste of ambrosia that clings to my tongue
Sweet fragrance that wafts through the air
Reminiscent of the days I truly felt young...
Sweet nectar that lingers over the heir as I ponder, and I think, I muse and I mind...
What is God's plan for ME?
What of ME, does he have in mind?

What IS God's plan... for me
As I tamper with the walkways of a narrow corridor
Dancing down the road least travelled
Stomping on the wooden floor, enacting the tribal dancing of my ancestors
Dancing the ancient rhyme of praise
Wood is a grounding place
Again, the vibrations moving through my soul to a language natural to me but forgotten
Speaking to the originator through words not spoken

the mind of a man

He's making love to my intellect again
His conversations always take me away
He is mind rocking me in ways I can't even begin to explain
He has me thinking everything twice over for days
I've come every time he strokes my membrane
He spits knowledge that you wouldn't even begin to understand
I wanna listen to his word daily
I want to be a part of his daily plans
I want more of his soul
I want to feel more of his spirit
I'm diving deeper and deeper into his physics
Learning as he flows
I don't care how much he talks
I just let him go
He talks of revelations
Of how the time is here
He talks of religion
How it divides and inputs fear
He speaks of war
And how the world as it stands will never know peace
He speaks of love and wanting to be free
He speaks of struggle
And will openly admit feeling caged as a man
Having the weight of providing for his family
And not knowing if he can
He speaks of the universe and the stars it fills
Wanting to be a part of them
He stares up at them every night still
He speaks of racism, war, and why people feel the need to kill
His words are powerful
They send chills down my spine

He is of divine design
When he speaks
I could feel the planets align
I want to walk with him
I want to follow the path he follows
I want to share his knowledge
Whatever he cooks up I'll swallow
He's a man of strong favor
Everyone looks at his behavior
Genetically modified to show Yahweh's labor
A man of strong character and will
The man that came after the savior

love like...

Undying, gratifying, eternal love
Love so deep, so spiritual
It can't really be spoken of
Love so powerful
So meaningful to us
Love stronger than power
Love greater than lust
I want this love to be something bigger than us
Love you can very well see
The love that only so few touch
Love that will withstand anger
That will form the foundation of trust
I want this love to understand forgiveness
I'm going to be selfish and say…
I want this love only for us
Love not based off greed
That will go on long after we've turned back to dust
That love I pray about
The love that lives in my dreams
Love that neither of us doubt
Love that never runs out
I want this love NOT to fog or cloud my judgement
But to free and ease my mind
I want this love never to wither
But to stand the test of time
Love to be my kingdom
And the beauty of it my throne
I want this love to be the beginning of the end
I want it to be like love I've never known

He was the stars in the night sky and the mist in the morning...

his faith

He looks at me as if his luck has finally changed
As if i was his last chance of hope
As if i was what his faith weighed

He opened up to me in ways i don't understand
Telling me about his struggles, his future, his plans
And why he chose to entrust me with information so personal,
I didn't think he considered me close
Anyone would be willing to hear what he says and to see how his life unfolds. He has such an interesting personality. He has an addicting soul.
I've liked him for so long, I didn't think it was reciprocal.
How could i have caught his eye?
Why try selling to me what you wish to buy?
It was beginning...
And what was beginning had begun
Fate, was in motion. A spiders web had been spun.

My disposition, a secret. I only wanted shared with him
He nourished my beliefs
He nourished my needs
exploding galaxies in his eyes, sown seeds he gave me
millenniums in his skin, proof of happiness and discipline
He's a discovery within discovery's embroidered and woven within the fabrics of his organic structure
He is a world of wonder
And Into his world i want to dive,
i want the plunder
The repercussions are worth the price of the sin
He looked at me as if his luck has finally changed… maybe it has

he is...

He's as sweet as honey and a savory as pie
He could make the blind see
a phenomenon
he was... is... always a phenomenon to me
my oxygen
he filled my soul
I couldn't get near without touching him
And when I touched him, I didn't want to let go
he was... is... my phenomenon
He'll always be a phenomenon to me
He satisfied my curiosity
He quenched my thirst
He fed the hunger in me
And in return I kept him first
He was... Is... My phenomenon, always a phenomenon to me
He's the horizon
The limit to limitless
He is perspective
The scope of actuality and utopia
Kindness lies in his eyes
My phenomenon, he was... Is... Always going to be
A phenomenon to me

He was the stars in the night sky and the mist in the morning...

my morning

He was the morning sun and the moon at noon
He was characterized by loyalty, voice and reason
Loved by all those who've seen him
He was the place my mind often visited and where my heart wanted to stay
He was the savior to the sinner
always the clear winner
and the motive behind my ambition
he was the sea i wanted to fish in
Transparency was his saving grace
god... You can see his work all over the place
he was the beginning and the end
my alpha and my omega
he was the test and the result
through all his teachings i never found one fault
to celebrate him is to celebrate life
he was the beginning of the day and the end at night
i say was as if he isn't here
as if he was but then disappeared
the truth is he never left
I'm just stingy
i want him all to myself
i keep him near
to me he's an exquisite priceless chandelier
and to him
I'm his personal pioneer

a flower in God's garden ...

He was someone on the inside
And i wanted to fit in
So i jumped when he said jump
I swam when he said swim
I saw him as a flower in God's garden
Or the forbidden fruit in the tree
The door i wasn't meant to go in
He was impermissible to me

My blessing opened my eyes and my heart, I found so much love in you...I hope I'm worthy of you

zion

Our bodies are a temple
designed to mimic Yahweh's center fold
A gene pool for the genes pulled
A navigational system from the spiritual world into the physical whirlpool
A shelf full of children ready to be made and fade into the life that apparently give us lemons to make lemonade
The literal hand of God
A life for which the angels prayed
Crafted, made and remade in the womb
Woven so neatly a camera lens wouldn't hold enough zoom
As overcrowded as the world is, so they say…
For this little one God still made room
A heritage foundation
Look at God's creation
Once kissed by light
First held in the twilight
His eyes clear the way
constellation in disarray
A blanket of love and protection placed on his right
I met strength and stayed up with him all night
Blessed with this joy
I'll never forget the day I first met my baby boy

the phoenix

What is a prodigy?
It is a mystery. An anomaly.
This particular prodigy was told
There is beauty in the struggle
I admit, when I first heard these words,
I had no idea what they meant.
How could there be beauty in difficulty, how could this be the essence of life's scent?
Will there be trouble following me?

A prodigy - from the ashes rose and made history
Into battle, then came victory
To ascend earth and race with the sun
A purified blessing has undone all its toil
You can see bits gold shining in the coal
There are bits of gold you can see in the soil
This must be the essence of life
Because how can you ever grow if you've never been to strife?

The scent of hope lingers
as the seekers of love Bring singers
And the favors of dancers enters solitariness as they speak to us through steps
and the lenders of movers direct us…
to certainty.
And the prodigy certainly, has plenty
Plenty of bruising from battle
Plenty emptiness from deprivation
Plenty isolation from quarantine
Through the embers of soot
The prodigy is reborn… with powers lent from the heavens
The resurrection.

Born of the sun.
Showing the threads of spiritual connection
With happiness coursing through my wings
I am the prodigy.
I am the mother of kings and queens.

you are...

You are a lifeline between beauty and grace, the moon rises and the sun sets each day more eager to see your face. A lifetime of fidelity and of truth, flawlessness anchored at your thighs, experience painted on your face and hands, a tale of wise sits in your eyes.

You are who you are.
A strength. Unorthodox. full and covered with scars, that sits so snuggly among the stars.

You are experience and memories.

Atoms and molecules.

You are oxygen.

You are the wings that soar on eagles.

You are who you are.

You are.

I said I want to give up. She said don't lose heart... but heart is all I have...

experiencing him

I need to Experience the stories of transferable energy
I feel like a garnish on his plate
Serving myself to a soulless invisible date
Making myself soulless
Emptying what fills me
Dirtying what cleans me
I've become an outlet for his rage
I am what makes him believe he is a man
I build his pride while I dim mine
I build his self-esteem while I bury mine

I fear

I fear if i loose him it'll be a chance I've missed
maybe i focus too much on the outer appearance than what enters me because this... This could be my one true chance of happiness, but I've thought this before.
Too many times I've liked someone, and I think this is it! wanting, craving, praying for more
but when it ends... I never feel like it's something I've missed and i never want to go back to that relationship,
but right now I'm in this turbo of emotions feeling like he's the one, finally I've awoken, I'm finally someone's someone.
I'm in the middle of thoughts, thinking I don't need love, but I'm happy I found it, although I'm good with it, I'm still good without it.
i found someone i connect with....
and this...this could be it...
I hope this one will last...
his energy is irresistible...
and I fear if i lose him, it'll be my last chance

He said those lips
Those eyes
Them hips
Oh and them thighs
I said, 'and what about my mind?'
And for this he had no response...

that's the way it goes

when did I stop self empowering?
I aimed to Identify with my own ego, now I question when I look at myself, where did she go?
Along with my confidence… where did I place my confidence?
did I bite more than I could swallow?
Thought when I grew up that life would be easy…
Instead I wonder aimlessly looking dreamy
Feeling like a shell of my former self
Waiting for someone, who's probably waiting for someone, who's probably waiting for someone else
That's how it always goes
When your waiting for someone, they're usually waiting for someone else
My self certainty has wavered
I have wavered

Before he left, I said to him, you are my world, you are my universe, you are my whole life. And before he left, his last words to me were that's a grand expectation

when love dies...

The love... it's filled with lies and no matter how many times I dry my eyes I still find new reasons to cry
And the multitude of my servitude for the man that knows nothing nor wants nothing at all
He who searches only for my intimacy while I hope after sharing myself I gain from him legitimacy
But the "gift", gestures rather small
Still I never want him to leave
But he never intends to stay
he never comes with a greeting or a smile that meets his eyes
But I'll still give him what he's needing and watch him whilst he gets ready to leave... again

I said I need for you to love me, he said you're asking for the impossible...

when he leaves...

Just because he ain't here doesn't mean he doesn't wanna be
The thing I constantly tell myself
Come into my nest, come.. I'll give you rest, come... lay your head upon my breast...
If only for one night
when he finally leaves, I all but try not to cry
when he leaves I stay in the spot where he once occupied
And when he leaves, whatever remains of him I amplify

He said she nor the situation meant anything to him, it's funny that, because it meant everything to me, and now I'm supposed to brush it off, this hiccup... this abnormality...

he left.

Before he left,
i thought nothing could break us,
nothing in the universe could tear us apart...

Before he left,
i felt on top of the world,
i loved him with all my heart...

Before he left, i hit the restart button, removed everyone and everything that didn't involve him...

Before he left, he said he'd never leave, that he'd forever be all i need before he left.

Before he left, an old friend of his came back into town, he said that SHE wanted HIM to show HER around...

Before he left, a person i never knew existed made more sense to him and became more important to him and became a pillar for all his decisions.

The night before he left, he said he never knew what he needed until her,

in my heart i pleaded, I wanted to know why her?... I wanted to say don't do this,
but my mouth never uttered a word. My lips never moved...
We both knew what he meant...
Because then...

I gave you

I gave you time
I gave you love
I gave you money
I gave you…
I gave you…
but what have you given me?

You deserve to be loved the same way you love
You deserve to be loved the same way you love

You deserve to be
loved the same way
you love
You deserve to be
loved the same way
you love
Remember that...

alive, wild and free

I educated my emittance and discovered she
Wondrous, bodacious, loud and silly
I became my very own self devotee
Me. Myself I see.
Alive, wild and free.

The voice of my father echoes through the tunnels of my years
"Queens are looked over, they have no place among the boys here"
Am i a queen?
Am i willing? More than able?
Do i not look for riches? Chase after labels?
Are my riches even Earthly?
Do I act accordingly?
I travel between my outlook and the waves of the ocean
I get so caught up in the motion
I've been told I'm forgetful in that way
But what I forget to tell myself is that I am worth so much more, more than what they tell me I am
I am worth some much more than anyone's opinions of me
I am worth so much more than they could ever understand
I am worth some much more because I am a part of God's plan
Me. Myself I see.
The alive the wild the free

where I want to be

I am not where I want to be
If I were, I'd imagine life to be moving by much more easily
I do wish that life worked differently
I wish that what I prayed for came as what I prayed for, tangible.
instead I get a lesson learned being something I change for

we forget

We've forgotten who we are
We've forgotten those that parted the seas and charted the stars
We've unremembered those that found multiple galaxies and multiple universes
Our memories have only gotten worse
Those that carved out the rivers, the oceans, the seas
Those that awakened us with a cool breeze brushed against us through the leaves and trees
We've lost connection with those that provide the morning
And gave us the moon
We've erased our caregivers
Our memories are as fleeting as the dessert sand
As fleeting as the forgotten forest that fades with the afternoon

alive and wild and...

I pray for Paradise while searching the light
On days I feel my ancestors' memories
I feel their memories mixed in with my own
And no, I'm not crazed
I'm emitting my own radiance, my own grace mixed in my own space
as I step through the portal depicting my own soul.
Me. Myself i see.
Alive and wild and free.

Embracing my Core
discovering my beginning
unearthing my truth
detecting my source
Identifying my reason
I am that gifted horse
I am that gifted season
I've travelled between plight and blessing
Honing in on my lessons
I've always looked for an ally
When who I've been searching for is me.
Me. Myself I see.
Alive and wild and free.

firefly

I am like a firefly
My butt lights up
I can purify, prophesy, unify any ambiguity with the strength of my own will, done by my own make up
I am wild
I am rare
Everything I do, I do through the power of prayer
I am the brainchild of an ancestors dream and a small-minded, overly opinionated persons nightmare
I am a firefly
I shine wherever I go
And wherever I go, I leave an echo

you

That golden brown
That natural crown
That glow
That same crown worn by so many ancestors not so long ago
That queen
That gene
Contemporary beauty blind to but once the eyes are opened can't be unseen

Lets just get a little real...and a little political

when they see us - one

When they see us? They see the enemy
You feel their hatred based off their energy
People tend to fear what they don't understand
And I get that... but when they see us?
I'll be damned. Don't they see murders, rapist, gang bangers
When we see them, do we see the Klan?!
But get mad when we say black lives matter, someone always shouts BUT ALL LIVES MATTER
Dressed up, button downed, served on a silver platter
You hear the chit chat, the titter tatter
'There goes the neighborhood'
When they see us? What do they see?
The news doesn't help, just creates newer enemies, or how about the fake 911 calls to the crazies.
That's what I call them, the crazies. You call them the pigs, the 5.0., the popo, all I know is they weren't built for my safety
Safety. Safety? When have you ever heard of a cop being a point you can reach safely?
And I know the news exaggerates and tell fatuous lies, people overreact, and for that people die
And I say it matter of factly because that's just how it is
I've become desensitized to the murdering's of black, the non white individuals
I've normalized the violence
And if I've become desensitized to it, what are we teaching the kids?
the bestiality spotlighted on my people, portrayed in films, Grotesque abstract appearance of the non white masquerading as a sadist
You can hear the come up of the carbon copy on the playlist
Mass media creates this image of misconceptions
And mass produces the fallacy of oppression
The tension always gets the attention

Always one extremist against the one peaceful protester
Always one aggressor to the one harmonious activist
Always one influencer the media prefers

we are

All this generation knows is common wealth
A land where you pay for good health
A land in which is governed by man but is always unmanned
Unsafe and unstable, and looks for no better future plans
We come from Pharaoh's and Queen's, nobilities, kingdom's
Repeated in stories
Seen in dreams
Our ancestors ruled and watched over everything
They gave us beginnings and showed us peace
We knew love
And love is what we released
And when our enemies tried to bury us for the blessings we received
They all but took our pride
Because a mountain that rest on a hill cannot hide
WE THE PEOPLE are the hill where mount Zion resides
WE THE PEOPLE harbor the infinite spirit
The dark brown to black pigmented
Dejected, devalued, dehumanized and defaced

They tried to mark our families in shame and disgrace
Tried to pin us down to being the worst of the human race
Our history still in tatters
Division still divides us
Yet still, with open arms and forgiveness
Our enemies we will still embrace
No. We don't consider those against us enemies
But those of whom are lost
So bare are witness to the miracles we gain
True witnesses of the Pentecost
We remember the pain
We just don't know who we are

when they see us - two

When they see us?
Do they see the future? Children are learning from the abuser
And I know that sounds dramatic
But the system is systematic
Methodical and calculated
It's undiplomatic, cinematic magic
Children are in awe
Their brains like sponges, soaking up everything they see and they run with
Growing up there was a willingness to embrace the naked definition of being a statistic
I believed that my environment was there to mold me
I grew up thinking all I saw was not to uplift but to hold me
Like how a mother cradles her child to protect it from harm, in fear if she lets it go, her baby will get harmed, but now I see I was being drowned in the bottom line of actuality
Because the dropout number was HIGH, and the pregnancy rating was HIGH, and the broken homes were HIGH, and the death toll amongst youths were HIGH, and many children got HIGH,
Aye! But as long as you looked fly
That was the motto when I was in HIGH school
Children of color are great consumers
Buy whatever your selling
The more expensive the better, look like, feel like, smell like we fresh to death
And death would and will greet some of us as we pour some more of that GREY GOOSE, while we lace up them TIM BOOTS, as we throw on that WHITE TEE, as we fold and rubber-band pack our MONEY
Yes! Fresh to death!
Just a bunch of broke individuals trying to feel important

Because When they see us?!...

you fear

You fear me
The mere mention of my name sends chills down your spine
You fear me
My anger you can't find so you find ways to try to demean me
Randomly searching me as if I fit the crime
Terrorized in my own home
Watch out! one time, one time
They beat you then shoot you but can't recall
what antagonizing words you've used that initiated the brawl
Blackout.
No, they wish to wash the black-out
The blacks are starting to standout
And stand up
Wake up!
No longer is the Shepherd needed
So long the dominate race has been undefeated
With their weapons of mass destruction
Every explosive leaving a new racial terror
A new introduction
To fear...
You fear me
My knowledge spreads further than your degree
Those brainwashing techniques no longer work on me
No strings on me
So, you fear me
You fear what I know
The truth.
How blacks were illiterate because they didn't use the language of the white man
How the kings and Queens before us stood too tall
So, you created the Klan
The truth

That there were 6 presidents before George Washington and Obama wasn't the first black one
The truth
That America is a land still stolen and built on the backs of slavery
The truth that America isn't United and a land of bravery
But a land built on fear
You fear me
You fear who I am and what I stand for and what I'm yet to become
You fear...

when they see us - three

When they see us,
They see those lazy bastards
Those of low standards, those cowards
They see those children of those ancestors
They see people who refuse to work for free
They see monkeys they refuse feed and don't want to leave
We are the individuals they don't want to unify
We are the individuals needed to build their homes, and to verify
They never wanted to share with us our labor
They brought and sold us, and tried to dethrone us
Hid our memories
We were glorious! Glorious! Glorious! servants,
but we were homeless
A people with no country,
A people with no plan
A people with no unity…
And like a Phoenix
we rose from the ashes
And representation has become everything to us
What our leaders before us tried to instill
Those in power wanted torn from us,
because when they see us?! They see Gods in the flesh
They see it In our melanin, our build, our hair, they see the truth carved into our chest
If history states that we were created in God's image
If we were made in the likeness of God
Then what have us little Gods allowed?
We have value, this younger generation is more boost-fully proud
Disciplined, educated, refined and cultured
Behind the vail, we are what we uncovered

We are what we discovered
We see value, we have value, we feel valued
We re-interrogated the curvatures relating to our identity
We've reached back to hold hands with the pharaohs, the kings and Nubian Goddesses
We see what the problem is
It's asking, when we look at OURSELVES, what do we see?
How do we define ourselves?
We've rivaled the past with the limitations we thought we had
We've re-edited our peoples legacy and made it our own

the black experience

What is freedom?
Are you free?...

We live in a world that makes it difficult to get ahead
we live in a time where its easier to get by when you're dead

we live in a place that doesn't want blacks to succeed,
prosper, flourish, advance or thrive
and despite the setbacks, we survive

what is privilege?
What is bondage?
What is freedom?
Are you free?

Or have you been held captive and developed Stockholm
syndrome, made yourself into a devotee...
enslaved to be made an accessory to the accusatory

they kill us. We die.
They sale to us false lies and we buy.
They set the rules and we comply.
They divide us and then crucify.

We exist in a place where churches are no longer safe
we exist in a time we die if we move, we die if we stay
we exist in a world where five-year old's say a prayer before
they enter the school gates

not knowing if today is the day they'll meet their maker, if some armed person will make them meet their fate

we survive
we experience
we black

we leave our homes not knowing what the day will hold
we leave our homes saying goodbye, might be the last goodbye you tell your household
we leave our loved ones not knowing if we'll make it back safely from work
we get in our car, on our bike, start our walk, moving fast, praying we don't run into a pig network.

We survive in a generation where everything is captured by moments
we survive after fighting in wars, sometimes by forced deployments
we survive with little victory and a lot of suffering, only to suffer at the hands of those who we've shed blood for.
We come back to worse suffering than before
we are conscious to a society that ignores the cries of the blacks, our netting unraveled on the police cells floor
bullets fly through the windows and the front doors, but not due to gang violence
but mistaken identity, you aren't the person and this isn't the house the police were searching for
but you met a description
and now your baby ain't breathing, and the police won't apologize, the most they'll get is ostracized
they'll be back to work in a month.

We exist
we expose
we black

we are living in a conscious society that chooses to live unconsciously
shaped by mental slavery, death to those who speak of change, because that shows bravery

everyone stay woke!

They want to break us, well… Can't break something that's already broke
broken families, broken homes, broken hearts to broken bones
killing one another instead of helping a brother

stay woke!

Ancestry teachings wiped away, made to believe that we were born only to be slaves
whipped, beaten and slaughtered for sport and to further evoke fear
something we see police do in 2018, the new KKK unclothed is here

self-reflection

I need to rectify...how I see me.
And just to clarify
I don't praise me nearly enough as I should. And i should…
praise my selfhood, my individuality, my value, my personality.
One upon a time I wanted A love to look at me amazingly
I wanted someone to marvel at my wonder
Collide their lightning with my thunder
They'll fill me with laughter and I'd drive away their hunger
They'd Sail the highs with my lows
I'd be their cosmos
But why should I look for love from people who don't yet know how to love themselves
Thinking the love I find will come with the love I find
In thinking this way, I have sidelined... me...
For who I was, who I am, who I'm still growing to be
That self doubt nested its home in the back of my mind beautifully
I question everything
Am I pretty? Am I enough? Does he like me? Should I give up?
That self doubt boy... that self doubt
Doubt will have you thinking you're not smart enough, you can't count, you'll never do it, after all this time, why reach out?

ABOUT THE AUTHOR

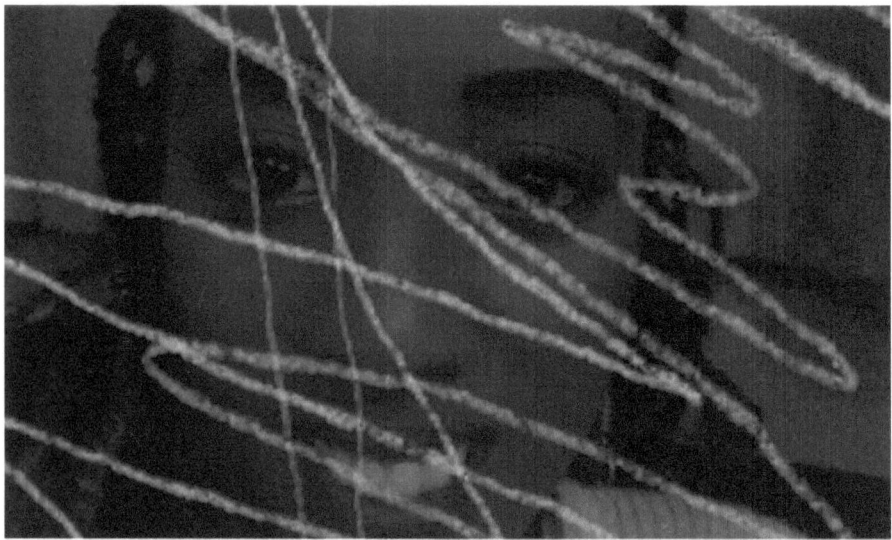

Sharnice is a mother as well as a poet and an artist. Sharnice has three degrees in various arts, scoping from sculpting, painting and drawing to photography and politics. This will be Sharnice's second published book. Her first publication being her port book called *Inspired by London.* Born in America, in Detroit, Michigan and now living in England, Sharnice has a unique view on how she interprets the world and of her experiences. She feels most free when she's writing poetry.

www.ingramcontent.com/pod-product-compliance
Lightning Source LLC
Chambersburg PA
CBHW030509220526
45464CB00006B/2719